NEW YEAR'S DAY

A TRUE BOOK

by

Dana Meachen Rau

Children's Press®

A Division of Grolier Publishing

New York London Hong Kong Sydney
Danbury, Connecticut

A mask worn for Chinese New Year

Reading Consultant
Linda Cornwell
Coordinator of School Quality
and Professional Improvement
Indiana State Teachers
Association

Author's Dedication
For the Runkels and
the Sanders

The photo on the cover shows a float in the Tournament of Roses Parade. The photo on the title page shows the ball that drops at midnight in Times Square.

Visit Children's Press® on the Internet at:
http://publishing.grolier.com

Library of Congress Cataloging-in-Publication Data

Rau, Dana Meachen
    New Year's day / by Dana Meachen Rau.
        p. cm. – (A true book)
    Includes index.
    Summary: Discusses the history, customs, and celebrations of New Year's Day.
    ISBN 0-516-21516-7 (lib. bdg.)   0-516-27062-1 (pbk.)
    1. New Year—Juvenile literature. [1. New Year. 2. Holidays.] I. Title.
II. Series
GT4905.R38 2000
394.2614—dc21   99–086740

GROLIER
PUBLISHING

Contents

Making noise is part of New Year's Eve fun.

Staying up Late

It's almost midnight. You may be up past your usual bed-time. The countdown begins: 10, 9, 8, 7, 6, 5, 4, 3, 2, 1, "Happy New Year!" Everyone cheers. You toss streamers or throw confetti. A new year has begun.

Some families play board games while waiting for midnight.

New Year's is the oldest holiday, and the only one celebrated by people all over the world. On New Year's Eve, many people stay up until midnight. On New Year's Day, families often gather together and think about the year to come. It is a time to ring out the old year, and bring in the new.

A Long History

The history of the holiday starts thousands of years ago. January 1 hasn't always been New Year's Day. Different cultures started their years on different days. The Egyptians started their year when the Nile River flooded. Other cultures started their year in

spring when plants started growing, or in autumn when plants were harvested. Some cultures based the start of their year on a certain phase of the Moon.

More than four thousand years ago, the Babylonians celebrated New Year's Day in March. Their parties lasted eleven days. Ancient Romans also celebrated in March, with grand parades and huge feasts. But in Rome, emperors often changed the calendar until it no longer was in line with the Sun and the seasons. In 45 B.C., Julius Caesar straightened things out. He declared January 1 the

beginning of the new year. January was named after Janus, a god of two faces. One face looked backward to the old year. The other face looked forward to the new one. Caesar's calendar is known as the Julian Calendar.

During the Middle Ages, different countries called different days the beginning of the year. Italy and France started the year in March. Spain and Germany started on

Peasants in a Belgian village enjoy a spring New Year celebration.

Christmas Day. Belgium and Holland started on Easter. Other countries started in autumn. It was often confusing for these countries to work together.

In 1582, Pope Gregory XIII fixed the calendar. He shortened

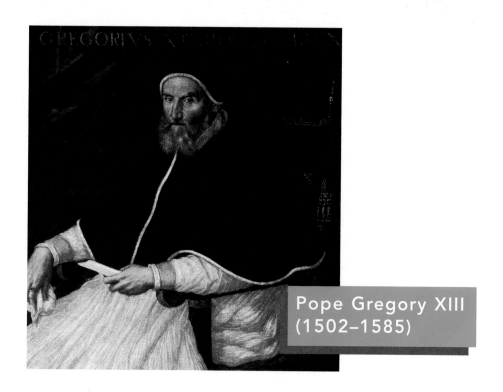

Pope Gregory XIII
(1502–1585)

the year by ten days and again
declared that January 1 was
New Year's Day. Not everyone
accepted the new calendar, how-
ever. England and its colonies
still used March 25 as the beginning of the year until 1752.

Good and Bad Luck

Ancient people believed that the old year had to be driven out with a lot of noise before the new year could arrive. The noise was meant to frighten away evil spirits who tried to bring bad luck into the new year. People in China used bells, whistles, firecrackers,

Children in Shanghai add sparklers to the noisy New Year street celebrations.

gongs, and guns. People today even honk their car horns when the new year arrives. In Denmark, it is a tradition to smash pottery against outside doors. The noise keeps evil spirits from crossing into the house.

Besides making noise, people used other ways to get rid of bad luck. In England, it was a tradition to leave all the doors open in a house so that the spirit of the old year could leave, and the new one could

Take your pick! Chinese masks hang on display.

enter. In China, wearing masks on New Year's Eve to hide smiling faces began as a way to confuse evil spirits. In Japan,

Laughing to welcome the new year is a tradition in Japan.

many people laugh to bring them good luck when the new year comes. Some people won't hang their calendars before New Year's Day so they won't bring last year's bad luck into the new year.

The New Year's Baby

A baby is a common symbol of the New Year. Some people say this idea began in Greece around 600 B.C. The Greeks placed a baby in a basket and paraded around the city. Other people say the tradition began in Germany in the 1300s. Wherever the tradition started, Baby New Year is a common New Year's character.

New Year's Traditions

Many traditions all over the world are an important part of New Year's celebrations. For some people, New Year's Day is a time to visit friends. In the 1800s, men called on women all day long. They would try to visit as many women as they could in one day. The

White House guests bow in greeting to George and Martha Washington.

women welcomed their visitors with delicious snacks. President George Washington and his wife Martha started the tradition of opening their house to anyone who wanted to visit.

American presidents continued having "open houses" on New Year's Day for many years.

Gift giving is also a New Year's tradition. Romans sent good-luck tokens to their friends. Egyptians gave flasks that symbolized good fortune. The British sent expensive gifts to their kings and queens. The Chinese have sent cards for more than one thousand years.

Today, in Greece, children often go from door to door

Greek-American children dance at a festival.

singing songs of good wishes for the year. In Spain, people try to eat twelve grapes before the first and last toll of the bell at midnight.

All around the World

Not everyone around the world celebrates New Year's Day on the same day. Some cultures still use their traditional calendars. The Jewish New Year, Rosh Hashanah, falls between September 6 and October 5. Muslims celebrate the new year on

At Rosh Hashanah,
the shofar is blown.

Hundreds of oil lamps are lit for the Diwali festival.

March 21. In parts of India, people celebrate Diwali, the Feast of Lights. Small lights, called chirags, are placed all over the houses and streets.

Chinese New Year takes place between January 21 and February 19 and lasts fourteen days. Dragons are a

A dragon joins this Chinese New Year parade.

A Chinese temple in California is decorated for the New Year.

symbol of good luck, so huge dragon puppets wind their way through the streets in large parades. In their homes, Chinese families hang red scrolls with good luck wishes printed on them. Chinese children receive coins in small red packets. On the last day of Chinese New Year, all of China glows with the light from lanterns.

Welcoming a New Year

How do you celebrate? Many people go out to see a show, listen to a concert, or eat at a restaurant on New Year's Eve. Some families rent movies and watch them until late at night. Most people try to stay up until midnight.

Does your family have a favorite movie to watch together on New Year's Eve?

Times Square is the scene for the world's largest New Year's Eve party.

For almost one hundred years, people have gathered in Times Square in New York City on New Year's Eve. The crowd watches a large, glittering ball drop down a pole as they count down to midnight. Almost two tons of confetti and balloons fly through the air and fireworks explode when the new year arrives. Even though it is not midnight at the same time all over the world, about three hundred million people watch the celebration on television.

The holiday is a time to be serious, too. People often make New Year's resolutions. These are promises to yourself that you try to keep for the new year. Someone might make a resolution to clean their room, make a new friend, or try to do better in school.

On New Year's Day, families often relax. Most people have the day off from work and school, so they use the time to have a nice meal or visit with

During Chinese New Year, this Malaysian-American family enjoys roast duck.

A surfer rides a wave of flowers in the Rose Parade.

family and friends. People may watch the Tournament of Roses Parade on television or

The Rose Bowl football game is played in Pasadena, California.

tune in to the Rose Bowl football game, which has been played since 1916.

In many parts of the world, church bells and fireworks "ring in the new."

People celebrate the coming of a new year in many different ways all over the world. New Year's Day is a time for everyone to say goodbye to the old year, and welcome all of the exciting things the new year will bring.

The Year

The whole world welcomed the arrival of the year 2000 with parties, light shows, and concerts.

The Red Square glows just after midnight.

People in New Zealand welcome the new year with a song.

2000

People of New Zealand were the first to see the New Year, at midnight on December 31, 1999. Every hour, as midnight hit other parts of the globe, each place had its own way of celebrating. The Eiffel Tower in Paris and St. Basil's Cathedral in Moscow's Red Square burst in bright displays of fireworks. What happened in your town or city?

Fireworks light up the Eiffel Tower (top). This woman (bottom) counts down the final seconds to the new year.

To Find Out More

Here are some additional resources to help you learn more about New Year's Day and other holidays:

 **Books**

Hoyt-Goldsmith, Diane. **Celebrating Chinese New Year.** Holiday House, 1998.

Sarnoff, Jane and Reynold Ruffins. **Light the Candles! Beat the Drums! A Book of Holidays.** Charles Scribner's Sons, 1979.

Sing, Rachel. **Chinese New Year's Dragon.** Little Simon Books, 1994.

Van Straalen, Alice. **The Book of Holidays Around the World.** E. P. Dutton, 1986.

Organizations and Online Sites

Chinese New Year
http://www.edu.uvic.ca/ faculty/mroth/438/CHINA/ Chinese_new_year.html

Learn about the celebration and its traditional foods, decorations, and customs.

Festivals.com
RSL Interactive
1001 Alaskan Way
Pier 55, Suite 288
Seattle, WA 98101
http://www.festivals.com/

Visit this site to find out about all types of festivals, holidays, and fairs around the world.

The Holiday Page
http://wilstar.com/holidays

Find out about your favorite celebrations at this site, which is devoted to holidays.

Important Words

colony a territory that has been settled by people from another country and is controlled by that country

confetti tiny, colorful pieces of paper

culture the way of life, ideas, customs, and traditions of a group of people

declare announce something formally

flask a small, flat bottle made to be carried in the pocket

resolution a promise to yourself

scroll a roll of paper

symbol an object that stands for something else

tradition a custom, idea, or belief that is handed down from one generation to the next

Index

Meet the Author

Ever since Dana Meachen Rau can remember, she has loved to write. A graduate of Trinity College in Hartford, Connecticut, Dana works as a children's book editor and has authored many books for children, including biographies, nonfiction, early readers, and historical fiction. She has also won awards for her short stories.

When Dana is not writing, she is doing her favorite things— watching movies, eating chocolate, and drawing pictures—with her husband Chris and son Charlie in Farmington, Connecticut.